20th CENTURY ORCHESTRA STUDIES

For Timpani

Compiled and Annotated
by **ALAN ABEL**

ED. 2741

G. SCHIRMER, Inc.

DISTRIBUTED BY

HAL•LEONARD®
CORPORATION

7777 W. BLUEMOUND RD. P.O. BOX 13819 MILWAUKEE, WI 53213

PREFACE

This series is designed to help both the student and the professional player towards a mastery of contemporary musical language and instrumental techniques. To attain this challenging goal, the writer-compiler of each book — a distinguished performer in his field — has chosen interesting, important passages from the symphonic literature of the 20th Century, accompanying many excerpts with special comments and suggestions concerning artistic and technical problems.

Extensive cueing is one of the special features of this series. Cues are used to indicate to the player how exposed the part is and what instrument he should listen for in order to be able to adjust in rhythm, volume and intonation to the ensemble of the orchestra. To indicate the place in the score where a given excerpt appears, the following system is used. A Roman numeral indicates the number of the movement; the rehearsal number or letter is followed by a number that indicates the number of bars between the rehearsal number (letter) and the excerpt. For instance, III $\boxed{B}$ + 12 indicates that the excerpt is in the third movement, 12 bars after letter $\boxed{B}$.

While the presentation of a complete, one-volume survey for each instrument is impossible, it is hoped, nevertheless, that this unique series will provide the player with a significant exposure to contemporary music along with the practical means to study it.

HENRY CHARLES SMITH, *Editor*

FOREWORD

This volume contains not only important excerpts from the timpani repertoire of the twentieth century, but also those which represent a variety of composers with contrasting styles. Every decade has representative works: Strauss in the early 1900's; Sibelius and Holst in the 20's; Stravinsky, Orff and Chavez in the 30's; Shostakovich, Hindemith, and Prokofiev in the 40's; Schuman, Carter, Bernstein, and Piston in the 50's; and Barber in the 60's. Much of the material is from the standard symphonic repertoire with a sampling of small orchestra pieces and unusual works.

Some of the most difficult problems encountered by the timpanist often involve a few isolated notes which are hard to tune perfectly, balance well, or play with the orchestra. There are excerpts which present these problems, but most of the passages have technical difficulties, are prominent and exposed, or are unaccompanied solos.

Many of the excerpts have printed tuning plans, which have been made with the understanding that a set of timpani will include four drums — 30″, 28″, 25″, and 23″, or their equivalents. Having fewer drums will perhaps necessitate a change in the plan. The types of drums (pedal, chain, cable, or hand-tuned) can also make a difference.

Other factors besides the normal tuning range of each drum were considered. When the dynamic marking is forte or above, each drum has a firmer sound in the middle to upper range, that is a fortissimo C sounds better on the 28″ drum than on the 25″. It is less hazardous to play technical passages on drums that are close together rather than wide apart. When there are many rapid tuning changes, it is often easier to keep track of the notes by keeping the outside drums (30″ and 23″) as stationary as possible with most of the tuning taking place on the inside drums (28″ and 25″).

No attempt has been made to suggest type and hardness of sticks except for general remarks made by the composer. There are too many variables to make it possible to recommend a specific stick for a certain passage; individuality in each timpanist's set of sticks, weather conditions, type and brand of timpani, individual taste, and conductor's preference.

A good timpanist will have a minimum of six pairs of sticks; some professional players have twenty or more. A musically sensitive timpanist will play a passage in rehearsal with several different pairs of sticks to determine which sounds best. Sometimes a knowledgeable colleague who takes a seat in the auditorium can be helpful, but be sure his musical tastes agree with yours.

Cues have been printed to help locate passages on recordings, and to insure secure entrances in performance. Some cues contain notes that will aid in checking tunings. Cue lines above certain excerpts should make ensemble playing more comfortable. It would be wise to use a metronome regularly in establishing correct tempos.

A.A.

CONTENTS

20th CENTURY ORCHESTRA STUDIES
FOR TIMPANI
Compiled and Annotated by Alan Abel

SAMUEL BARBER
Medea's Meditation and Dance of Vengeance

SAMUEL BARBER
Piano Concerto

* Since the piano is usually on the edge of the stage and the timpani are at the back, the timpanist has a "built in" time lag unless he accurately anticipates the beat.

Gb, Bb, D, Gb

III Con grazia, come prima

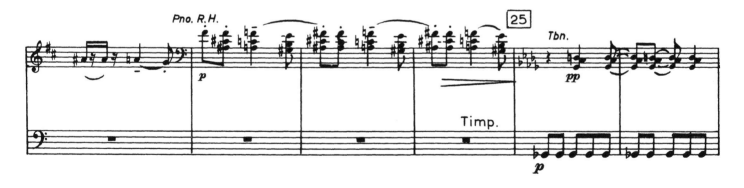

4

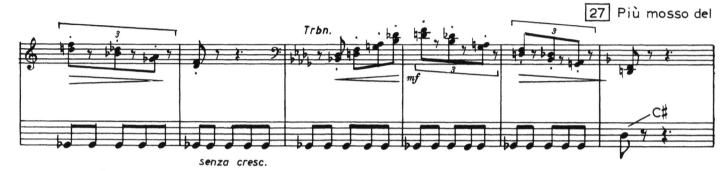

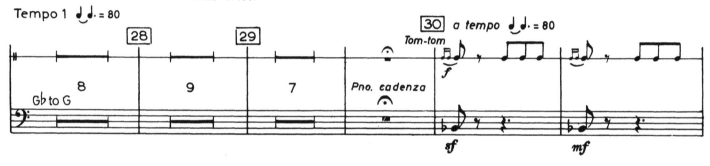

SAMUEL BARBER
Second Essay for Orchestra

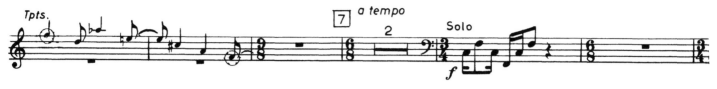

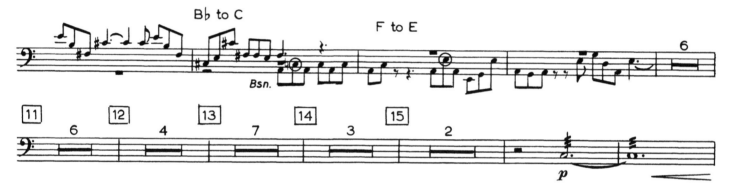

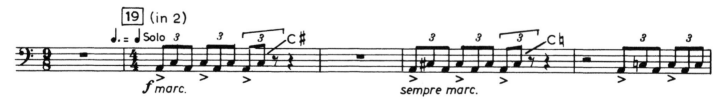

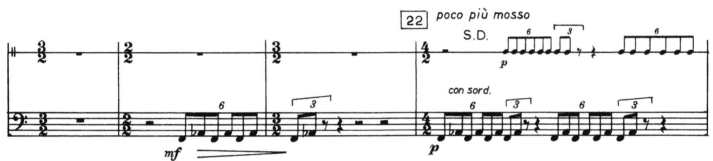

SAMUEL BARBER

Toccata Festiva

LEONARD BERNSTEIN

Overture to "Candide"

LEONARD BERNSTEIN

On the Waterfront

* If there are enough timpani available, it is preferable that these two notes (1. B♮ and B♭, 2. G and F♯) be played on two separate drums.

LEONARD BERNSTEIN
The Age of Anxiety (Symphony No. 2)

Here the timpani part is very exposed. Timpani, percussion, harp, celeste and string basses accompany the piano solo.

THE MASQUE

BORIS BLACHER
Orchester Ornament

* Number of eighth-notes in a measure.

BORIS BLACHER

Variations on a Theme of Paganini

VAR. 16 E,B,D

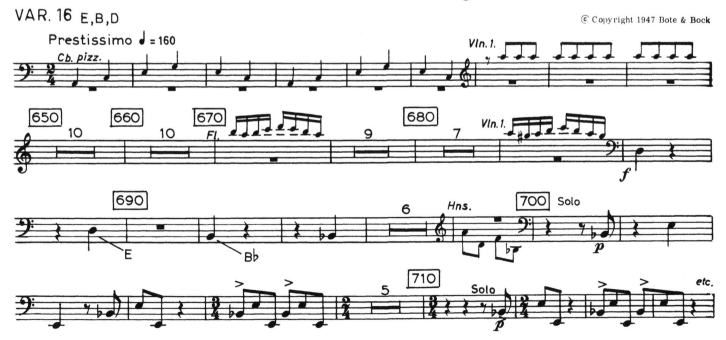

ELLIOTT CARTER
Variations for Orchestra

* Principal theme

CARLOS CHAVEZ
Sinfonia India

PAUL CRESTON

Invocation and Dance

ROY HARRIS

Third Symphony

KARL AMADEUS HARTMANN
Symphony No. 6

Six Timpani - No tuning plan is printed. There are too many variables such as available drum sizes, etc.

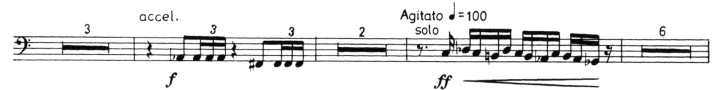

19

20

cresc.

cresc.

cresc.

cresc.

pochiss. meno mosso

etc.

pp

II [270] ♩ = 176
sehr virtuos (with virtuosity)

etc.

ff   ff   ff   ff

II [387] ♩ = 176
Solo

ff   ff   ff

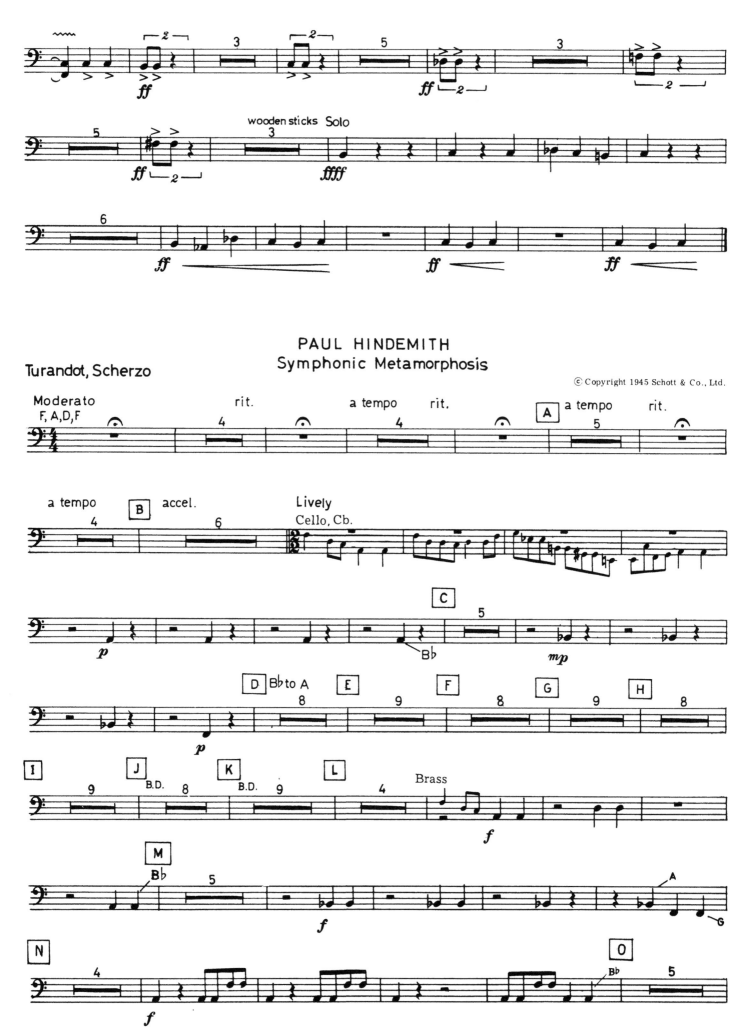

PAUL HINDEMITH
Symphonic Metamorphosis

Turandot, Scherzo

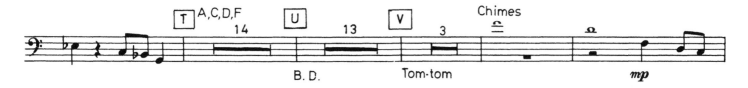

poco   a   poco   dim.

mf dim.

3

p   dim.

pp

GUSTAV HOLST
The Planets

IV Jupiter

Allegro giocoso
A,B,C

6 Timpani
2 Players   11
G,D,E

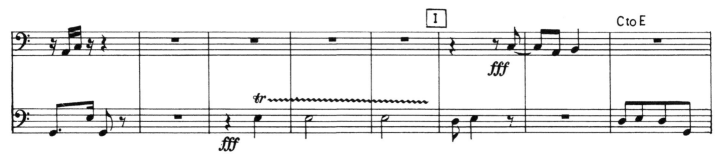

Timp. 2

Timp. 2

VI stringendo
(Timp. 2)

Più mosso

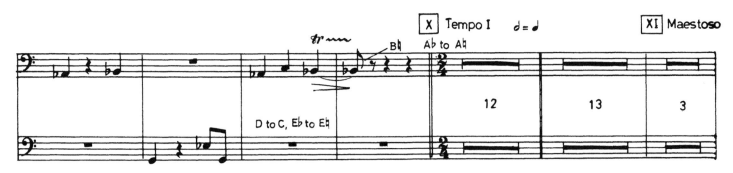

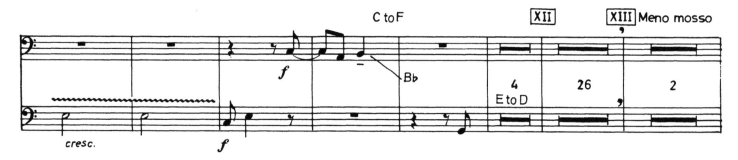

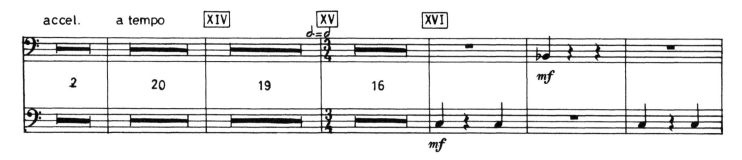

VI. Uranus

Allegro

Timp. I G, B, Eb, F, Timp. II F#, C

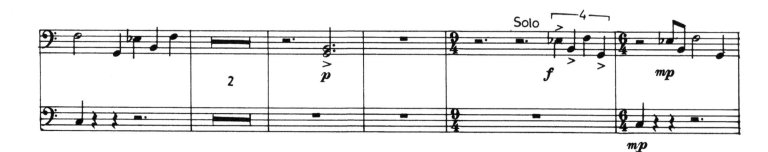

DMITRI KABALEVSKY
Overture "Colas Breugnon"

Articulation is important.

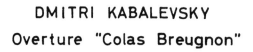

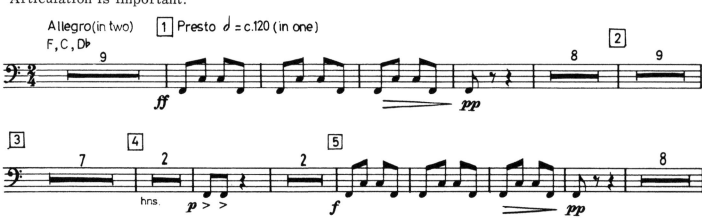

29

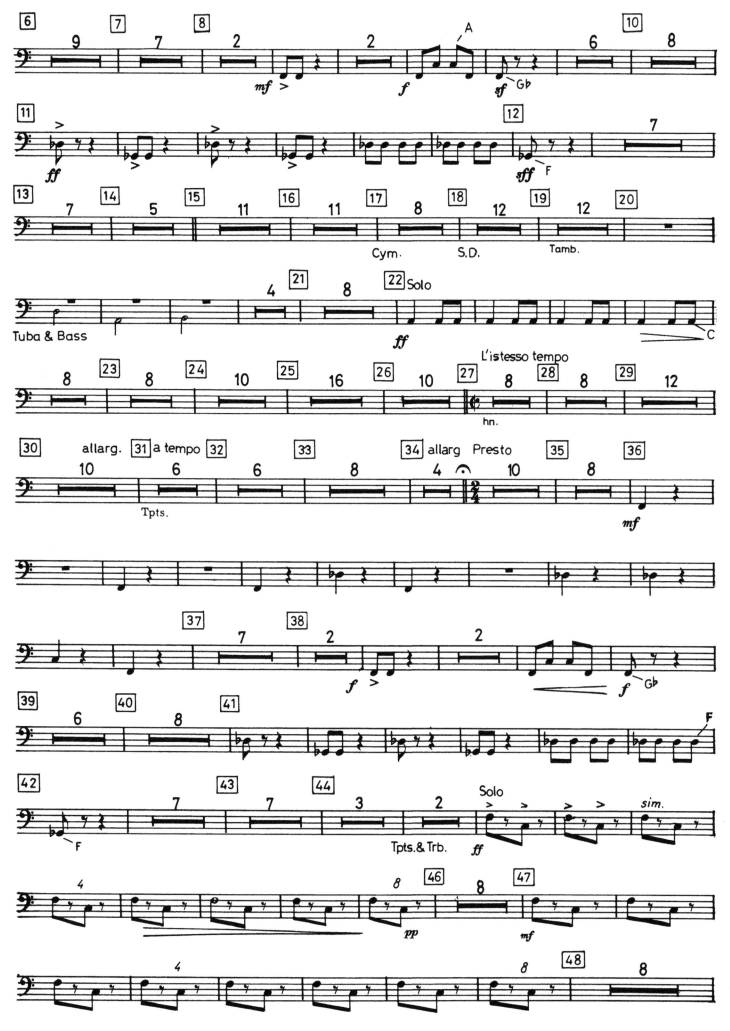

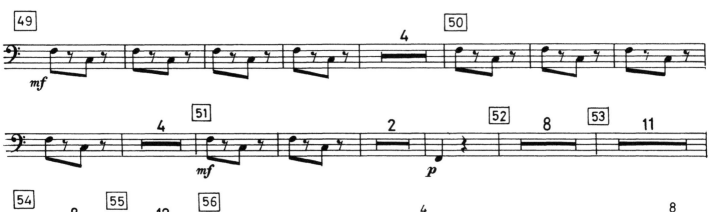

CARL NIELSEN
Symphony No. 4

49

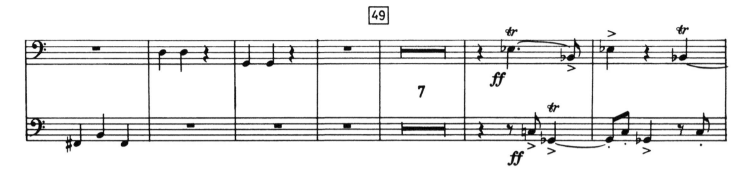

58 L'istesso tempo (in 1)

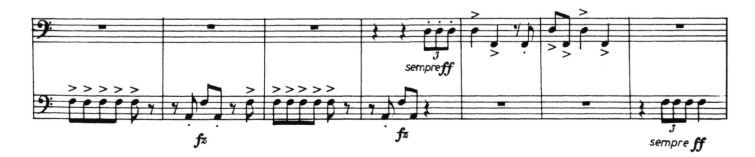

34

CARL ORFF
Carmina Burana

I. O Fortuna

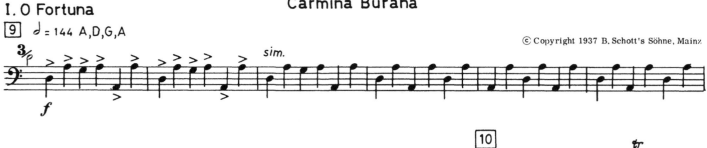

5. Ecce gratum

7. Floret silva

22. Tempus est iocundum

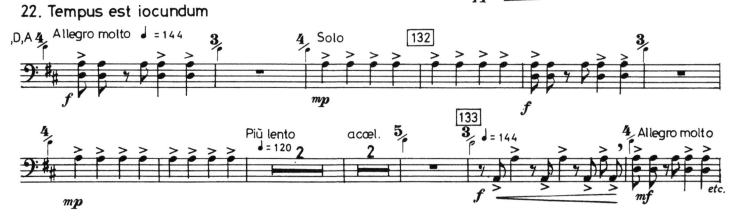

WALTER PISTON
Fourth Symphony

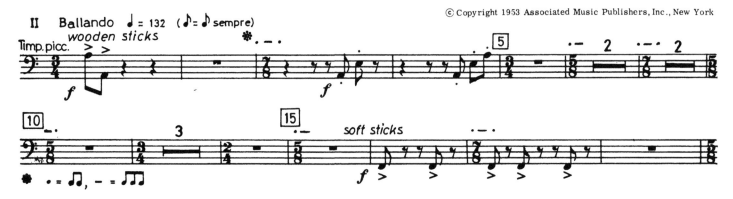

37

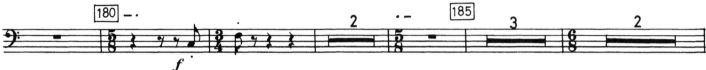

SERGEY PROKOFIEV
Classical Symphony

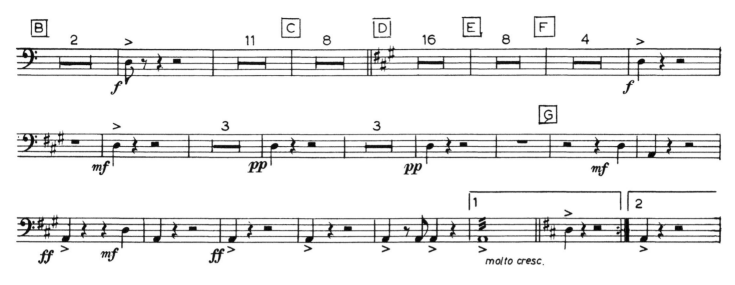

SERGEY PROKOFIEV
Sixth Symphony

III [60] Vivace

A♭,B♭,E♭,F

III [116] Andante

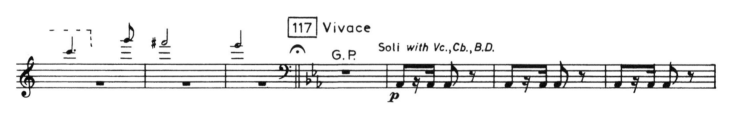

SILVESTRE REVUELTAS
Sensemayá

WILLIAM SCHUMAN
Judith

WILLIAM SCHUMAN
New England Triptych

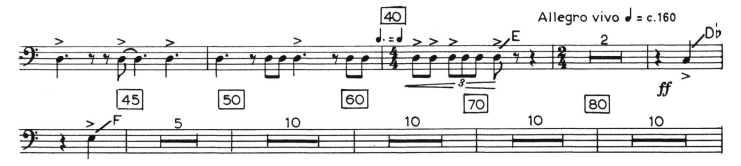

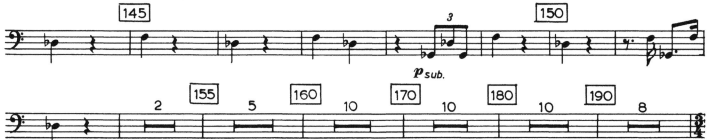

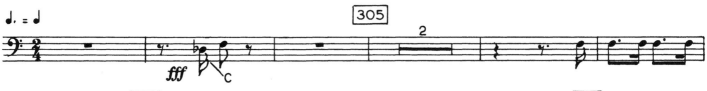

WILLIAM SCHUMAN
Sixth Symphony

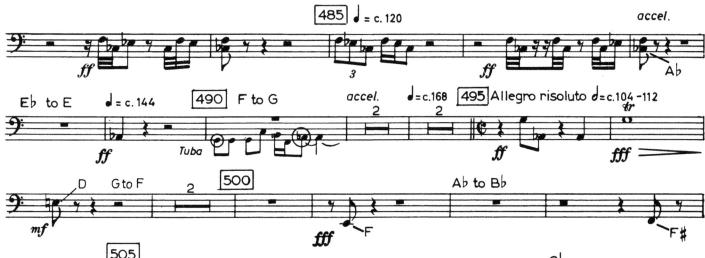

DMITRI SHOSTAKOVICH

Sixth Symphony

16   Tpt.

pp

etc.

I 26 ♩=52

Vln.1.

poco rit.

a tempo

F♯ B C D   E♭

p

D

ppp

trem. 27

etc.

II 65 Allegro ♩=88-96

Xyl.

G,A,E♭   66

ff

Trb.3.

poco rit.

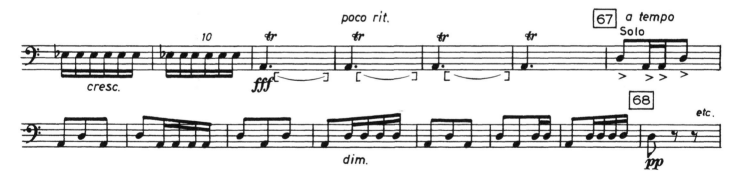

10   tr   tr   tr   tr

67 a tempo
Solo

cresc.

fff

68

etc.

dim.

pp

II 80 +1 ♩=88-96

Hns.

81 Solo
coperti

p

etc.

48

DMITRI SHOSTAKOVICH
Seventh Symphony

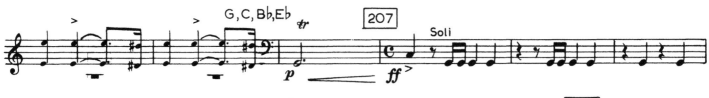

JEAN SIBELIUS
Seventh Symphony

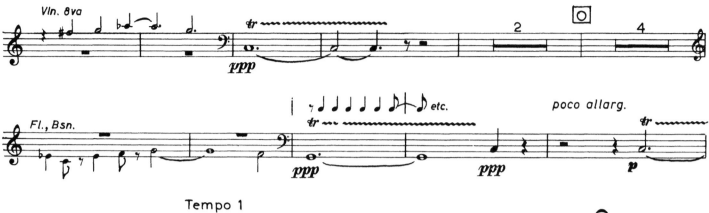

RICHARD STRAUSS

Don Juan

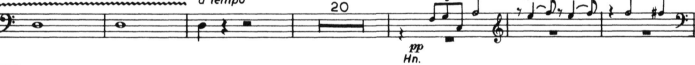

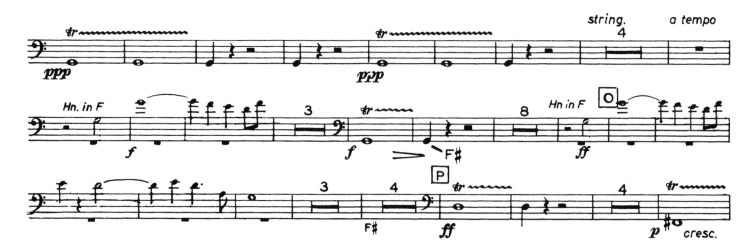

RICHARD STRAUSS

Salome's Dance

Pauken and kleine Pauke combined.

Sehr schnell und heftig (Presto con forza)

59

IGOR STRAVINSKY

Jeu de Cartes

TROISIÈME DONNE

IGOR STRAVINSKY

The Rite of Spring

62

JEUX DES CITÉS RIVALES

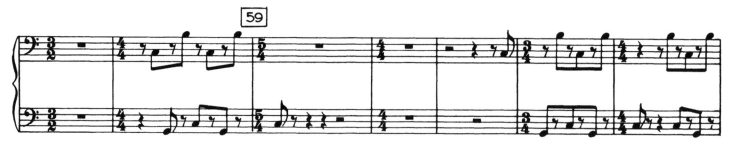

GLORIFICATION DE L'ÉLUE

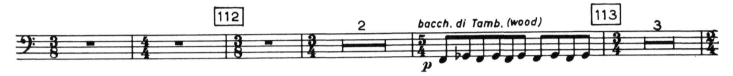

EVOCATION DES ANCÊTRES

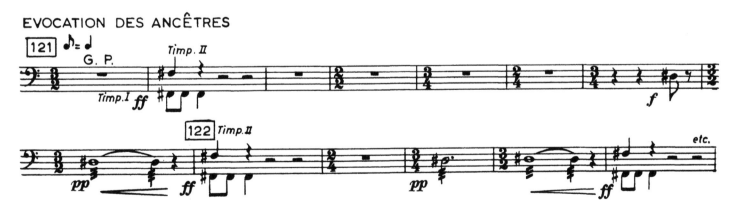

ACTION RITUELLE DES ANCÊTRES   DANSE SACRALE

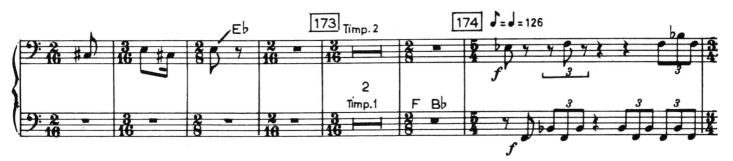

* E♭ sometimes played by Timp. 1

JAROMIR WEINBERGER

Polka and Fugue
from "Shvanda"

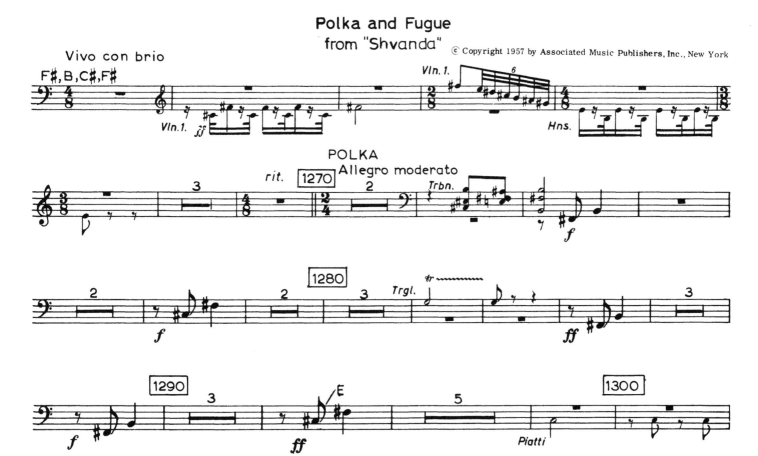

68

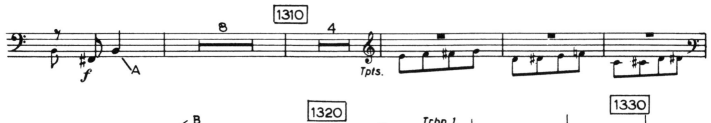

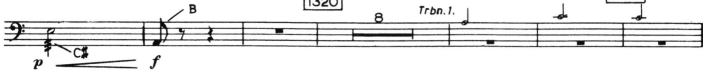

FUGUE
Allegro   F♯ to A, B to C♯,
     Tacet C♯ to E

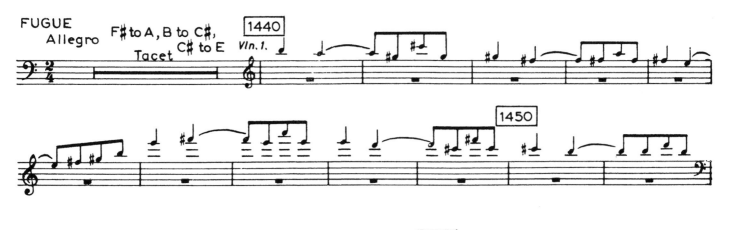

poco a poco cresc.